Gooseberry Patch

cake mixes

Classics

One of the secrets of a happy life
is continuous small treats.
—Iris Murdoch

Sugar-Topped Muffins

18-1/4 oz. pkg. white cake
   mix with pudding
1/2 t. nutmeg
1 c. milk

2 eggs
1/3 c. sugar
1/2 t. cinnamon
1/4 c. butter, melted

Blend cake mix, nutmeg, milk and eggs on low speed of an
electric mixer until just moistened; blend on high speed for
2 minutes. Fill paper-lined muffin cups 2/3 full; bake at
350 degrees until golden, about 15 to 25 minutes. Cool for
5 minutes; remove from muffin cups to cool completely.
Combine sugar and cinnamon on a small plate; set aside. Dip
muffin tops into butter; roll in sugar and cinnamon mixture.
Serve warm. Makes 2 dozen.

For a little extra sweetness, drizzle a powdered sugar
glaze over Sugar-Topped Muffins. It's easy...just
add 2 tablespoons milk to 1-1/2 cups powdered
sugar; blend until smooth.

Lemon-Poppy Seed Muffins

18-1/4 oz. pkg. white cake
   mix
6-oz. pkg. instant lemon
   pudding mix

2 T. poppy seed
3 eggs
1-1/4 c. water
1/3 c. oil

Combine the first 3 ingredients in a large mixing bowl; set aside. Whisk remaining ingredients in a medium mixing bowl; gradually blend into the dry ingredients. Fill paper-lined muffin cups 2/3 full; bake at 350 degrees for 20 minutes or until a toothpick inserted in the centers removes clean. Cool for 5 minutes; remove from muffin cups to cool completely. Makes about 1-1/2 dozen.

Enjoy the taste of freshly made muffins any time!
Freeze baked muffins in a freezer-safe bag, then just
remove as many as needed and let thaw
in the refrigerator overnight.

Brown Sugar Breakfast Rolls

3 pkgs. active dry yeast
2-1/2 c. warm water
18-1/4 oz. pkg. white cake
    mix
4-1/2 c. all-purpose flour,
    divided

1/2 c. butter, softened
1/2 c. brown sugar, packed
2 t. cinnamon
1/4 c. butter, melted
1/3 c. sugar

Dissolve yeast in warm water in a small bowl; set aside until creamy, about 10 minutes. Combine cake mix, 3 cups flour and yeast mixture; stir well. Mix in remaining flour 1/2 cup at a time; knead until smooth, about 8 minutes. Place in a greased bowl, turning to coat both sides; cover with a damp cloth and set aside until double in bulk. Punch dough down; roll out on a lightly floured surface into a 16"x10" rectangle. Spread with softened butter; sprinkle with brown sugar and cinnamon. Roll up jelly-roll style beginning with a long edge; cut into one-inch slices. Whisk melted butter and sugar together; dip top of each roll into sugar mixture. Arrange in a greased 13"x9" baking pan; cover and let rise until double in bulk. Bake at 350 degrees until golden, about 20 minutes. Makes 16.

A basket filled with the Sunday paper, a thermos of chilled orange juice or steaming hot coffee and a batch of Brown Sugar Breakfast Rolls will be a welcome early-morning delivery!

Pumpkin Coffee Cake

2 16-oz. pkgs. pound cake
   mix
4 t. pumpkin pie spice
2 t. baking soda

3/4 c. water
15-oz. can pumpkin pie
   filling
4 eggs

Combine the first 3 ingredients; add water, pie filling and eggs, blending well. Pour half the batter into a greased 13"x9" baking pan; sprinkle half the topping over the batter. Spread with remaining batter; add remaining topping. Bake at 325 degrees for 50 minutes. Serves 15 to 18.

Topping:

3/4 c. brown sugar, packed
3/4 c. chopped walnuts

1/2 c. all-purpose flour
1/3 c. chilled butter

Toss ingredients together until crumbly.

Sprinkle some candy corn over the Pumpkin Coffee Cake topping for a delightful Halloween surprise!

Cinnamon-Filled Pudding Cake

18-1/4 oz. pkg. yellow cake
   mix
3.4-oz. pkg. instant vanilla
   pudding mix
3/4 c. oil
3/4 c. water

1 t. vanilla extract
1/2 t. butter flavoring
4 eggs
1/4 c. sugar
1-1/4 t. cinnamon

Combine first 6 ingredients in a large mixing bowl. Blend in eggs, one at a time, until mixture is smooth; set aside. In a separate bowl, combine sugar and cinnamon; sprinkle half in a greased Bundt® pan. Pour half the cake batter in pan; sprinkle remaining cinnamon-sugar mixture on top. Pour remaining batter on top. Bake at 350 degrees for one hour or until golden. Allow cake to cool for several minutes before removing from pan; drizzle icing over top while still warm. Serves 12.

Icing:

1 c. powdered sugar
3 T. milk

1/4 t. butter flavoring

Mix all ingredients until smooth and creamy.

Tin picnic baskets, popular in the 1940's and 1950's are stylish and perfect for keeping sweet treats fresh while toting to any get-together.

Butterscotch Cake

18-1/4 oz. pkg. yellow cake
   mix
15-3/4 oz. can butterscotch
   pie filling

3 eggs, beaten
2 c. butterscotch chips

Combine first 3 ingredients together; mix well. Spread in a greased 13"x9" baking pan; sprinkle with butterscotch chips. Bake at 350 degrees for 35 to 40 minutes or until a toothpick inserted in the center removes clean. Serves 12.

Chocolate Chip-Pudding Cake

3-1/2 oz. pkg. cook & serve
   chocolate pudding mix

18-1/4 oz. pkg. chocolate
   cake mix
2 c. chocolate chips

Prepare pudding mix according to package directions; remove from stove. Stir in cake mix until just moistened; spread in a greased and floured 13"x9" baking pan. Sprinkle with chocolate chips; bake at 325 degrees for 30 to 35 minutes. Makes 14 to 16 servings.

Mix 'em up! Add variety to cake recipes by substituting raspberry, chocolate-mint or peanut butter chips.

Pound Cake in a Hurry

18-1/4 oz. pkg. white cake
   mix
1 c. sour cream

3-1/2 oz. pkg. instant vanilla
   pudding mix
4 eggs
1 c. oil

Blend all ingredients together; pour into a greased and floured Bundt® pan. Bake at 350 degrees for 45 to 50 minutes. Makes 10 servings.

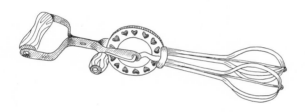

Whipped Topping Pistachio Cake

18-1/4 oz. pkg. white cake
   mix
2 3-1/2 oz. pkgs. instant
   pistachio pudding mix,
   divided
3 eggs

1 c. lemon-lime soda
1 c. oil
1 c. chopped pecans, divided
1-1/2 c. cold milk
2 c. frozen whipped topping,
   thawed

Combine cake mix, one package pudding mix, eggs, soda, oil and 1/2 cup pecans; mix well. Spread in a greased and floured 13"x9" baking pan; bake at 350 degrees for 40 minutes or until a toothpick inserted in the center removes clean. Set aside to cool. Blend remaining pudding mix and milk together; fold in whipped topping. Spread over cooled cake; sprinkle with remaining pecans. Refrigerate for one to 2 hours before serving. Makes 10 to 12 servings.

Angel Strudel

1 c. butter
2 c. all-purpose flour
3 egg yolks
2 T. vinegar
1/4 c. water

1 c. ground walnuts
1 c. chopped maraschino
   cherries
16-oz. pkg. angel food cake
   mix

Cut butter into flour using a pastry cutter; set aside. Combine egg yolks, vinegar and water together; blend into flour mixture. Divide dough into quarters; wrap in plastic wrap and refrigerate overnight. When ready to prepare strudel, combine walnuts, cherries and cake mix; divide into 4 equal portions and set aside. Roll out one section of dough into a very thin rectangle on a lightly floured surface; spread with one portion cherry mixture. Roll up jelly-roll style; place on an ungreased baking sheet. Repeat with remaining dough and filling. Bake at 325 degrees for 25 minutes; cut each roll into 6 slices. Makes 2 dozen.

Cherries and chocolate are always a winning combination.
Try topping individual servings of Angel Strudel with
chocolate glaze and a maraschino cherry.

Lemon-Lime Cake

18-1/4 oz. pkg. lemon cake
  mix
3-1/2 oz. pkg. instant lemon
  pudding mix

3/4 c. oil
12-oz. can lemon-lime soda
16-oz. container cream
  cheese frosting

Mix first 4 ingredients together; spread into a lightly greased
13"x9" baking pan. Bake at 350 degrees for 40 minutes. Cool;
spread with frosting. Refrigerate until ready to serve. Makes
15 to 18 servings.

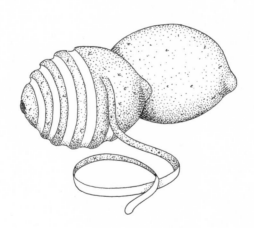

Do you know someone who loves to bake? Fill a
fabric-lined basket or mixing bowl with all the
ingredients to a favorite cake mix recipe. Tuck in a
spatula and tie on the recipe for an oh-so-welcome gift!

Peach-Berry Cobbler

18-1/4 oz. pkg. yellow cake
   mix
1/2 t. cinnamon
1/4 t. nutmeg
1 c. butter, softened
1/2 c. chopped nuts

21-oz. can peach pie filling
16-oz. can whole-berry
   cranberry sauce
vanilla ice cream or frozen
   whipped topping, thawed

Combine first 3 ingredients in a large mixing bowl; cut in
butter with a pastry blender until coarse crumbs form. Stir in
nuts; set aside. Mix pie filling and cranberry sauce together
in an ungreased 13"x9" baking pan; sprinkle cake mixture
on top. Bake at 350 degrees for 45 to 50 minutes. Serve
over ice cream or top with whipped topping to serve. Makes
16 servings.

Oh-So-Peachy Cake

18-1/4 oz. pkg. yellow cake
   mix
3-1/2 oz. pkg. instant vanilla
   pudding mix
4 eggs
1 c. water
1 c. oil

29-oz. can sliced peaches,
   drained and juices
   reserved
1 c. sugar
8-oz. pkg. cream cheese,
   softened

Combine first 5 ingredients; mix well. Spread in a lightly
greased 13"x9" baking pan; arrange peach slices on top. Set
aside. Blend sugar, cream cheese and 5 tablespoons reserved
peach juice together until smooth and creamy; pour over peach
slices. Bake at 350 degrees for 50 minutes. Makes 12 to
15 servings.

Oatmeal-Raspberry Bars

18-1/4 oz. pkg. yellow cake
   mix
3/4 c. butter, melted
2-1/2 c. quick-cooking oats,
   uncooked

12-oz. jar raspberry jam
1 T. warm water

Combine cake mix, butter and oats in a large mixing bowl;
toss until crumbly. Press half the mixture firmly into the
bottom of a greased 13"x9" baking pan; set aside. Stir jam
and water together; spread evenly over crust layer. Cover with
remaining crumb mixture, patting firmly over the top; bake at
375 degrees for 20 minutes. Drizzle with glaze while warm.
Cool; slice into bars to serve. Makes 15 to 18.

Glaze:

1 c. powdered sugar

warm water

Combine powdered sugar with enough warm water until a
desired drizzling consistency is reached.

To easily remove bar cookies, line the baking pan with
foil leaving 3 inches hanging over each end. Then, use
the foil to lift out the treats...easy cleanup too!

Gooey Cherry-Mallow Squares

4 c. mini marshmallows
18-1/4 oz. pkg. yellow cake
   mix

21-oz. can cherry pie filling

Spray the bottom of a 13"x9" baking pan with non-stick vegetable spray; arrange marshmallows evenly in pan. Prepare cake mix according to package directions; pour over marshmallows. Spoon pie filling on top; bake at 350 degrees for 45 to 50 minutes. Cool and cut into squares to serve. Makes 15 servings.

Rhubarb Cobbler

4 c. rhubarb, chopped
1 c. sugar
18-1/4 oz. pkg. white cake
   mix

3-oz. pkg. strawberry gelatin
   mix
1 c. water
1/3 c. butter, melted

Layer the first 4 ingredients in the order listed in an ungreased 13"x9" baking pan; pour water and butter on top. Do not stir. Bake at 350 degrees for 45 to 60 minutes. Makes 15 to 18 servings.

Sweet & Simple Rainbow Cake

16-oz. pkg. angel food cake
  mix

red, blue, yellow and green
  food coloring
Garnish: powdered sugar

Prepare cake mix following package directions; do not pour
into tube pan. Place one cup batter into each of 4 different
bowls; tint one pink, one blue, one yellow and one green.
Spread pink batter into a greased and floured tube pan;
carefully spoon blue batter on top. Repeat with yellow and
then green batters; carefully place on lowest rack of oven,
baking according to package directions. Remove from oven;
invert onto a serving platter. Let cool; sprinkle with powdered
sugar. Serves 10.

Try this tip for easy removal when cooling angel food
cakes...invert the tube pan on a funnel or over
the neck of a soda pop bottle.

Delicious Strawberry Angel Roll

16-oz. pkg. angel food cake
   mix
1 qt. strawberries, hulled
   and sliced

1/4 c. sugar
2 c. whipping cream
3 T. powdered sugar

Prepare cake mix according to package directions; pour into a greased jelly-roll pan lined with wax paper. Bake at 375 degrees for 10 to 12 minutes. Turn cake onto a towel dusted with powdered sugar. Peel off wax paper. Starting at narrow end, roll up cake and towel together; cool on wire rack for 20 minutes, seam-side down. In a mixing bowl, combine strawberries and sugar; set aside. In a separate bowl, blend cream until foamy; gradually add powdered sugar, mixing until soft peaks form. Drain strawberries. Unroll cake and remove towel. Spread with half the whipped cream mixture; top with strawberries. Re-roll cake; place on a plate seam-side down. Serve with remaining whipped cream mixture. Serves 10 to 12.

Try filling Delicious Strawberry Angel Roll with frosting, pie filling or puréed fruit...all yummy variations on the original recipe!

Peanut Butter & Chip Cookies

2 eggs
1/3 c. water
1/4 c. margarine, melted
1-1/2 c. creamy peanut
   butter
1-1/2 c. brown sugar,
   packed
18-1/4 oz. pkg. yellow cake
   mix, divided
2 c. chocolate chips

Blend eggs, water, margarine, peanut butter, brown sugar and half the cake mix together until smooth; stir in remaining cake mix and chocolate chips. Drop by rounded tablespoonfuls onto ungreased baking sheets. Bake at 375 degrees for 10 minutes. Makes 4 to 5 dozen.

BIG Chocolate Cookies

2 18-1/4 oz. pkgs. chocolate
   cake mix
16-3/4 oz. pkg. brownie mix
3 eggs
3/4 c. oil
3/4 c. water

Combine all ingredients together; drop by tablespoonfuls 3 inches apart on ungreased baking sheets. Bake at 325 degrees for 8 to 10 minutes. Makes about 6 dozen.

Lollipop Cookies

18-1/4 oz. pkg. vanilla cake
  mix
1/3 c. oil
2 eggs

10 to 24 wooden popsicle
  sticks
16-oz. container favorite
  frosting

Combine cake mix, oil and eggs; drop by rounded tablespoonfuls 3 inches apart on ungreased baking sheets. Insert top inch of a wooden popsicle stick into each mound of dough; bake at 375 degrees for 8 to 10 minutes. Cool completely; spread with frosting. Makes about 2 dozen.

A lollipop bouquet! Fit florists' foam into a new terra cotta pot and slip Lollipop Cookies securely into the foam. Cover the foam with colorful crinkled paper...what a kid-pleasing treat!

Orange Cream Cake in a Cup Mix

18-1/4 oz. pkg. white cake
  mix
3.4-oz. pkg. instant vanilla
  pudding mix
16 plastic zipping bags
2-2/3 c. powdered sugar,
  divided

12 t. unsweetened orange
  drink mix, divided
8 12-oz. microwave-safe
  coffee mugs

Place cake mix and pudding mix in a large bowl; blend well
with a wire whisk. Place 1/2 cup dry mix into each of
8 bags; smooth each bag to remove as much air as possible
before sealing. Label each bag "Cake Mix." Place 1/3 cup
powdered sugar and 1-1/2 teaspoons drink mix into each
remaining bag; label "Glaze Mix." Place one of each mix
into each mug. Attach a gift tag with instructions to each
mug. Makes 8.

Instructions:

Generously coat inside of mug with non-stick vegetable spray.
Empty Cake Mix into mug. Add one egg white, one tablespoon
oil and one tablespoon water; stir well until combined.
Microwave on high for 2 minutes. While cake is baking, place
Glaze Mix into a small bowl; add 1-1/2 teaspoons water and
mix well. Pour glaze over warm cake.

Make-Your-Own Chocolate Cake Mix in a Jar

3 c. all-purpose flour
2 c. sugar
2 t. baking soda

3 T. baking cocoa
2 t. salt

Sift ingredients together; pack into a one-quart, wide-mouth jar. Secure lid; attach instructions.

Instructions:

Place mix in a large mixing bowl; make 3 wells in mixture. Pour one teaspoon vanilla extract into one well, 3/4 cup oil into another and 2 tablespoons white vinegar into the last well. Pour 2 cups cold water on top; mix well. Spread in an ungreased 13"x9" baking pan; bake at 350 degrees for 30 to 40 minutes or until a toothpick inserted in the center removes clean. Serves 10 to 12.

For a spin on the traditional college student care package, fill a new 10-gallon galvanized garbage can with lots of snacks and these quick & easy mixes. Use pressure-sensitive stick-on letters to spell "junk food" on the outside of the can...what a rescue package at exam time!

Heavenly Black Forest Cake

18-1/4 oz. pkg. devil's food
  cake mix
3 eggs
21-oz. can cherry pie filling

1 t. vanilla extract
1 T. sour cream
3/4 c. milk
Garnish: chocolate chips

Combine all ingredients in a large mixing bowl; mix well. Spread into a greased Bundt® pan; bake at 350 degrees for 45 to 55 minutes. Turn out onto a serving plate; cool. Frost and sprinkle with chocolate chips before serving. Makes 12 to 15 servings.

Frosting:

3.4-oz. pkg. instant vanilla
  pudding mix

8-oz. container frozen
  whipped topping, thawed

Prepare pudding mix according to package directions; fold in whipped topping. Mix gently until combined.

Instead of sprinkling with chocolate chips, gently press toasted almonds over Heavenly Black Forest Cake...an irresistible variation for almond lovers!

Raspberry-Hazelnut Chocolate Torte

18-1/4 oz. pkg. chocolate
    cake mix
10-oz. jar raspberry jam

1 c. chopped hazelnuts,
    toasted
Garnish: powdered sugar

Prepare cake mix according to package directions; pour equally into 2 greased 9" round baking pans. Bake according to package directions; cool completely. Slice each layer in half horizontally, making 4 thin cake layers; set aside. Melt raspberry jam in a small saucepan over low heat; cool slightly. Place one cake layer on a serving plate; spread with one third of the raspberry jam. Sprinkle with one third of the hazelnuts; top with another layer, spreading one third jam and sprinkling one third nuts on top. Repeat with third layer. Arrange fourth layer on top; sprinkle with powdered sugar. Serve immediately. Makes 8 to 10 servings.

Use what professional bakers do when making tortes...a length of dental floss to cut a cake into even layers!

Snowballs with Cranberry Sauce

18-1/4 oz. pkg. white cake
   mix

Prepare cake mix according to package directions; pour equally
into 8 greased custard cups. Cover each tightly with aluminum
foil; place in a deep baking pan filled with one inch warm
water. Carefully place in a 325-degree oven; steam for
25 minutes. Remove from oven; turn out of cups onto
individual serving plates. Spoon cranberry sauce on top; serve
warm. Makes 8.

Cranberry Sauce:

1 c. sugar   2 c. cranberries
1 c. water   1 T. cornstarch

Heat sugar and water in a 2-quart saucepan until sugar
dissolves; stir often. Add cranberries; heat until skins burst.
Mix in cornstarch; bring to a boil, stirring constantly.

Snowballs with Cranberry Sauce are ideal desserts for
any holiday dinner. Look for custard cups with
frosty wintertime designs to make the
table even more festive!

Mini Eggnog Cakes

1/2 c. ground walnuts,
    divided
18-1/4 oz. pkg. yellow cake
    mix
1 c. eggnog

1/4 c. oil
3 eggs
2 T. orange juice
1/4 t. nutmeg

Equally divide walnuts into the bottoms of 12 greased and floured one-cup Bundt® pans; set aside. Blend remaining ingredients together for 2 minutes; fill each Bundt® pan half full. Bake at 350 degrees for 10 to 25 minutes; cool on wire racks for 15 minutes. Remove from pans and cool completely. Makes one dozen.

Fill the centers of Mini Eggnog Cakes with a dollop of homemade whipping cream or pipe some around the edges of each cake...so delicious and easy! Just beat together 3 cups chilled whipping cream and 1/3 cup powdered sugar until stiff peaks form.

Chocolate Spice Cake

18-1/4 oz. pkg. German
   chocolate cake mix
1-1/2 t. cinnamon

3 eggs, beaten
12-oz. can date pie filling

Combine cake mix and cinnamon; add eggs and pie filling, stirring until just moistened. Spread in a greased tube pan; bake at 350 degrees for 55 minutes to one hour. Cool; remove from pan. Serves 12.

Upside-Down Pecan Loaf

3/4 c. butter, melted
1 c. brown sugar, packed
2 c. pecan pieces

1/4 c. corn syrup
18-1/4 oz. pkg. yellow cake
   mix

Combine first 4 ingredients; divide and spread equally into 2 greased and floured 9"x5" loaf pans. Set aside. Prepare cake mix according to package directions using 2 tablespoons less water; divide and pour equally into loaf pans. Bake at 275 degrees for 55 to 60 minutes; carefully invert pans immediately onto rimmed serving plates. Let stand for 2 minutes; remove pans. Slice and serve warm. Makes 16 servings.

Nut Roll Bars

18-1/4 oz. pkg. yellow cake
  mix
1/4 c. butter, melted
1 egg
3 c. mini marshmallows
2 c. peanut butter chips

1/2 c. corn syrup
1/2 c. butter
1 t. vanilla extract
2 c. chopped peanuts
2 c. crispy rice cereal

Combine cake mix, melted butter and egg; press into an ungreased 13"x9" baking pan; bake at 350 degrees for 10 to 12 minutes. Arrange marshmallows on top; bake 3 additional minutes. Melt chips, corn syrup and butter in a double boiler; stir in vanilla. Mix in peanuts and cereal; spread over marshmallow layer. Refrigerate until firm. Makes 2 dozen.

Mmmm...for those peanut butter and chocolate lovers,
place unwrapped peanut butter cup candies on top of
Nut Roll Bars right after adding the warm glaze.

Fun Bars

18-1/4 oz. pkg. chocolate
 fudge cake mix
1/4 c. butter
1/4 c. water

1 egg
3 c. mini marshmallows
1 c. candy-coated chocolates
1/2 c. pecans

Combine cake mix, butter, water and egg together; mix well. Press into a greased 13"x9" baking pan; bake at 375 degrees for 20 to 24 minutes. Sprinkle with marshmallows, candy-coated chocolates and pecans; bake until marshmallows melt, about 2 to 3 minutes. Cool completely; cut into bars to serve. Makes 1-1/2 to 2 dozen.

Speedy Little Devils

18-1/4 oz. pkg. devil's food
 cake mix
1/2 c. margarine, melted

3/4 c. creamy peanut butter
13-oz. jar marshmallow
 creme

Blend cake mix and margarine in a large mixing bowl; remove 1/2 cup mixture and set aside. Press remaining mixture into a lightly greased 13"x9" baking pan; set aside. Mix peanut butter and marshmallow creme together; spread over cake mixture in pan. Sprinkle reserved cake mixture on top; bake at 350 degrees for 20 minutes. Cut into bars to serve. Makes one to 1-1/2 dozen.

Caramel Layer Brownies

14-oz. pkg. caramels,
 unwrapped
2/3 c. evaporated milk,
 divided
18-1/4 oz. pkg. German
 chocolate cake mix

3/4 c. butter, melted
1 c. chopped nuts
1 c. semi-sweet chocolate
 chips

Heat caramels and 1/3 cup evaporated milk in a heavy
saucepan, stirring until melted and smooth; set aside. Combine
cake mix, butter, remaining evaporated milk and nuts; mix
until just moistened. Press half of cake mixture into the bottom
of a 13"x9" baking pan that has been sprayed with non-stick
vegetable spray; bake at 350 degrees for 6 minutes. Sprinkle
with chocolate chips; spread caramel mixture over the top.
Flatten pieces of remaining dough with your hands and place
over the caramel layer; bake for 15 to 18 minutes. Cool
slightly; refrigerate for 30 minutes to firm caramel layer. Cut
into bars to serve. Makes 3 dozen.

Adding chocolate curls
dresses up any dessert
and they're a snap to
make...just pull a vegetable
peeler over a chocolate
bar and refrigerate
curls until needed.

Cookies & Cream Cake

18-1/4 oz. pkg. white cake
   mix
1-1/4 c. water
1/3 c. oil

3 egg whites
1 c. chocolate sandwich
   cookies, crushed

Combine cake mix, water, oil and egg whites in a large mixing bowl; blend until just moistened. Blend on high speed with an electric mixer for 2 minutes; gently fold in crushed cookies. Divide and pour equally into 2 greased and floured 8" round baking pans; bake at 350 degrees for 30 minutes or until a toothpick inserted in the center removes clean. Cool for 10 minutes; remove from pans to a wire rack to cool completely. Frost. Serves 12.

Frosting:

4 to 4-1/2 c. powdered sugar
1/2 c. shortening

1/4 c. milk
1 t. vanilla extract

Blend all ingredients together until smooth and creamy.

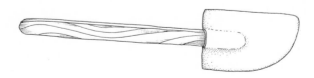

Place a stencil over frosted cakes or cookies and shake a can of sprinkles, jimmies or baking cocoa over the stencil to make a quick & easy design!

Root Beer Cake

18-1/4 oz. pkg. white cake
  mix
2-1/4 c. chilled root beer,
  divided

1/4 c. oil
2 eggs
1 env. whipped topping mix

Blend cake mix, 1-1/4 cups root beer, oil and eggs together; spread into a greased 13"x9" baking pan. Bake at 350 degrees for 30 to 35 minutes; cool completely. Blend remaining root beer and whipped topping mix together until soft peaks form; frost cake. Makes 24 servings.

Easy Ice Cream Sandwiches

18-1/4 oz. pkg. chocolate
  cake mix

4 c. vanilla ice cream,
  softened

Mix cake mix according to package directions, omitting eggs. Drop by tablespoonfuls onto greased baking sheets; bake at 350 degrees for 15 minutes. Cool completely. Spread ice cream on the flat bottom side of half the cookies; top with remaining cookies, flat-bottom side down. Gently press to form a sandwich; wrap individually in plastic wrap. Freeze. Makes 6 servings.

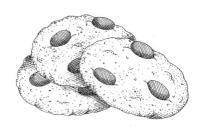

	Cake Mix	Vanilla Extract	Oil	Butter
			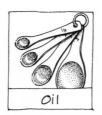	
Devil's Food	+		1/2 c.	+
Angel Food	+	1 t.		+
German Chocolate	+		1/2 c.	+
Yellow			+	1/4 c. +
Yellow	+		1/4 c.	+

$1 + 1 = $ Fun!

Use this handy formula to make your favorite cookies using standard cake mixes. Math was never so fun and tasty! Just roll dough into balls, place 2 inches apart on ungreased baking sheets and bake at 375 degrees for 10 to 12 minutes.

Eggs	Water	Other	Your Cookie
2	+	1 c. chocolate chips	= Chocolate-Chocolate Chip
	1/2 c. +	2 c. coconut	= Coconut Meringue
2	+	1 c. chocolate chips 1/2 c. oats	= German Chocolate Chip
2 +	1/3 c. +	1-1/2 c. peanut butter 1-1/2 c. brown sugar	= Peanut Butter Chip
2	+	1 t. cinnamon 1/2 c. sugar	= Snicker-doodles

YUM!

2 + 2 = More for You!

Index

Angel Streudel..9
BIG Chocolate Cookies..16
Brown Sugar Breakfast Rolls.....................................4
Butterscotch Cake..7
Cake Mix Cookie Math...30-31
Caramel Layer Brownies..27
Chocolate Chip-Pudding Cake...................................7
Chocolate Spice Cake...24
Cinnamon-Filled Pudding Cake.................................6
Cookies & Cream Cake...28
Delicious Strawberry Angel Roll..............................15
Easy Ice Cream Sandwiches.....................................29
Fun Bars..26
Gooey Cherry-Mallow Squares................................13
Heavenly Black Forest Cake.....................................20
Lemon-Lime Cake...10
Lemon-Poppy Seed Muffins.......................................3
Lollipop Cookies...17
Make-Your-Own Chocolate Cake Mix in a Jar...........19
Mini Eggnog Cakes...23
Nut Roll Bars..25
Oatmeal-Raspberry Bars..12
Oh-So-Peachy Cake..11
Orange Cream Cake in a Cup Mix.............................18
Peach-Berry Cobbler...11
Peanut Butter & Chip Cookies..................................16
Pound Cake in a Hurry...8
Pumpkin Coffee Cake...5
Raspberry-Hazelnut Chocolate Torte........................21
Rhubarb Cobbler..13
Root Beer Cake...29
Snowballs with Cranberry Sauce..............................22
Speedy Little Devils..26
Sugar-Topped Muffins..2
Sweet & Simple Rainbow Cake.................................14
Upside-Down Pecan Loaf..24
Whipped Topping Pistachio Cake...............................8